SALFORD AS IT WAS

Alan Smith, A.L.A.

Reference and Local History Librarian, Salford Public Libraries.

Front Cover—Flat Iron Market 1894. A photograph by S. L. Coulthurst.

Published by: Hendon Publishing Company Limited, Hendon Mill, Nelson, Lancashire.
Text © Alan Smith 1973
Printed by: Fretwell & Brian Ltd., Howden Hall, Silsden, Keighley, Yorkshire.

90p

Introduction

SALFORD, perhaps more than most cities, has undergone enormous changes in recent years, and in this book I have assembled what seems to me interesting and diverse illustrations of its past. This is a personal selection, and I am well aware of the important omissions which such a selection is bound to entail. I hope that the book will afford the reader some small measure of the enjoyment which I have found in compiling it.

All the photographs are from the extensive collection in the Local History Department of Salford Public Libraries which has been built up by the generosity of many people over a number of years. The library is constantly seeking to enlarge its resources and will always be very happy to receive donations of photographs or loans for copying. I am most grateful to Miss D. N. Pearce, the Salford City Librarian for her kind permission to reproduce the illistrations in this book, and to all the public-spirited people who have made gifts or loans of material.

My especial thanks are due to Edward Gray, Chris Makepeace, Derek Seddon, Mrs. Barbara Knott and Mrs. J. Peters for their invaluable help and kindness.

At the heart of old Salford was Greengate, and no building in that street was more famous than the Bull's Head, a mediaeval timbered inn with an unusual south gable built on crucks. It was reputed to be the oldest licensed house in England; certainly it had been an inn for more than 600 years when it closed in 1930. In 1931 the brewers offered to present the building as a free gift to Salford Corporation, but sadly this offer was rejected. Fire damaged it in February 1937, and it was finally demolished just before the last war. This photograph shows the inn in about the year 1907, looking strong and immovable enough to endure for another 600 years.

On the opposite side of Greengate, and facing the Bull's Head stood these old houses. When this photograph was taken in 1898 they were obviously in a terminal decline, and were indeed demolished in 1901, but their overhanging, Tudor-style upper storey gives a clear indication of their very considerable age. Greengate was by now a very poor area, as is shown by the shabby spectators who stare fascinatedly at the camera. The little boy whose face appears at the elbow of the street hawker has obviously jumped along the pavement, leaving a set of ghostly images of himself. This was one of the penalties of the slow speed films of the time.

Chapel Street in 1878—a most interesting photograph showing the buildings which clustered at the bottom of Victoria Bridge Street. The Old Ship Hotel had long been established, and there is still a public house of the same name on the site, which replaced the one destroyed by enemy action in the last war. The half-timbered building, part of which was known as the Fisherman's Hut, is now believed to have been the remains of the original Salford Hall.

A back view of the Fisherman's Hut, the front of which is shown on the previous page, not long before its demolition in 1894. It owed its name to its closeness to the Irwell, and during its life as a hall would have had pleasant gardens sloping down to the river. All its former glories had departed by 1894, however, and its mediaeval origins would have been of little comfort to its impoverished occupants.

Flat Iron Market in 1894. A photograph by S. L. Coulthurst, another example of whose work appears on the front cover of this book. Coulthurst was an exponent of the completely unposed photograph, and to achieve this end he would go about the streets with his camera concealed in an old clothes cart. This is a beautiful example of his art. The formidable character who faces the camera and who is obviously the proprietor of a second-hand boot business, surveys his prospective customers with undisguised suspicion.

Time moves on at the Flat Iron Market. This view of it was taken in July 1925. It owed its unusual name to the three streets, Gravel Lane, Chapel Street and Blackfriars Road which formed a triangle rather like the base of an old fashioned flat iron round the church of Sacred Trinity. In this triangle the market had been held for several centuries when it was officially closed in June 1939 at the same time as the new Cross Lane Market was opened. Most of the buildings shown here are little changed today.

The New Bailey Prison, which was opened in 1790 and demolished in 1871 was the major prison in this area until the opening of Strangeways Jail in 1868. It stood on the site of Salford Station goods yard. at the junction of New Bailey Street and Stanley Street. Although it was felt to be a model prison at the time of its construction, it looks a grim enough place in this print of 1829, with a macabre and massive pair of fetters hung over its main entrance in Stanley Street. There were several public executions here including those of the Fenians—Allen, Gould and Larkin in 1867. The site of the Lying-in Hospital and Deaf and Dumb School on the left of the picture is now occupied by the Ralli building.

On this page we see views too early for the camera to have recorded. This was Salford Cross which stood on the town green at the junction of Greengate, Gravel Lane and what is now New Bridge Street. In 1747 John Wesley preached here and was roughly handled by a crowd of his opponents. This picture dates from not long before its dismantling in 1824.

Salford Town Hall is still standing, of course, but this engraving of it dates from the pre-photographic year of 1831. It was built in 1827, and originally used as a market building. but was bought by the Salford Commissioners of Police for £3,000 in 1834.

The Town Hall did not retain its dignified semi-isolation for long. A warren of streets soon grew up around it, and many of these have only recently been cleared away. This photograph, the most recent in the book, jumps forward to 1929. Crowded and close the houses may have been, but there is a marvellously infectious enthusiasm in this picture of children's games in Cleminson Street played against a back-cloth of the Town Hall and the tower of St. Stephen's Church.

The Pendleton Fire Engine of 1864. At that time Salford's fire services were under the jurisdiction of the police, and the dignified gentleman in top hat at the foot of the picture is the police-inspector in charge of the fire-fighters.

Not the Victorian forerunners of the Keystone Cops, but the Salford Fire Brigade in the year 1890. This highly individual form of transport appears to have been an experimental change from the conventional horse-drawn fire engine of the time. It was obviously inspired by the phenomenal popularity of the bicycle, but not surprisingly it does not seem to have been an unqualified success.

The most important main road in Salford at one time was the River Irwell. This picture shows the Albert or New Bailey Bridge and landing stage in 1890, when boats such as this carried passengers regularly to and from Warrington and Runcorn. The bridge was built in 1844 and is still a busy connection between Salford and Manchester. The remains of the landing stage can also be seen.

This was Broughton Suspension Bridge which was opened in 1826. It connected Pendleton with Broughton and was considered a notable engineering achievement. Unfortunately the bridge collapsed while the 60th Rifle Corps was marching over it on April 12th 1830 and 60 men were thrown into the Irwell, 6 of these being very seriously injured. It was subsequently repaired and finally dismantled in 1914, to be replaced in 1924 by the Gerald Road footbridge on the same site. This photograph of the 1890's was taken from the Broughton bank.

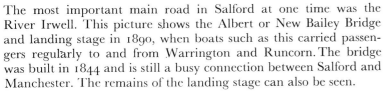

The river was also a source of recreation. It was used by several rowing clubs and there were annual regattas. Here a solitary oarsman enjoys the peace of the Irwell near Peel Park in about the year 1890. The windmill, the remains of which can be seen on the far shore stood near the site of the present Salford University footbridge.

A horse-drawn omnibus stops for passengers at the Victoria Arch entrance to Peel Park in 1866. This oriental looking structure, reminiscent of the Brighton Pavilion, was built in 1860 to commemmorate the second visit of Queen Victoria to Peel Park in 1857. Traffic vibration eventually rendered it unsafe, however and it was taken down in July 1937.

A very different conveyance from that of 1866. This was the first Salford Corporation bus, photographed on its maiden trip on July 5th 1920 in Great Clowes Street. Mr. Harry Berry, the conductor, who stands beside it shows a very obvious and understandable pride in the vehicle.

Bury New Road in April 1902. The electric tramways had arrived in the previous year, but it still seems very much a horse-drawn world. The large house is 'Adswood', which is still standing although now shorn of some of its timbering and without its distinctive turret.

By 1919 however, the motor vehicle was offering serious competition to the slower horse and cart in the transportation of goods. This mixed fleet lined up outside Rothwell's Wholesale Grocers, Cannon Street in that year shows a sensible combination of the old and the new.

Eccles New Road in the early 1920's. This important thoroughfare was opened in 1827 and runs straight as a Roman road and parallel to the Manchester Liverpool railway which came into being in 1830. The crowded tram and the large number of men walking towards Cross Lane indicate that these may be football supporters on a Saturday afternoon. Alternatively it could be the regular Sunday walk along the road, which older residents will remember as the 'Monkey Parade'. The large gaunt building on the left is the Salford Workhouse, built in 1852 and demolished in 1926 to make way for the Langworthy Estate Flats. The shops on the right remain virtually unchanged.

The interior of the Eccles New Road Workshouse in 1900. A rare and fascinating glimpse of what life was like for the orphan and foundling. A stark and cheerless existence, no doubt, but these young inmates were at least fed and clothed and spared the worst privations of many children outside its walls.

It comes as a shock to realise that this is a girls dormitory in the workhouse. The shaved heads were considered essential to combat vermin, but the effect of this practice on a girl's sense of femininity can well be imagined. In all fairness it must be added that an attempt has obviously been made to brighten up the dormitory with pictures, even though these would doubtless have been of an improving and high moral tone.

Taylorson Street School, Ordsall in 1910. The bare impoverished classroom could hardly have inspired a thirst for knowledge in the minds of these rigidly attentive young scholars. Once again close-cropped hair, at least for the boys is considered advisable in the interests of hygiene.

A much more pleasing picture of Salford children. In Lower Seedley Road girls dance round a portable maypole and elect their May-Queen. The year is 1914 and folk customs such as this were fast disappearing from Salford life.

Lark Hill, a superbly situated mansion, was built in 1790. It was the home of Colonel Ackers of the Manchester and Salford Volunteers and later of William Garnett. It became the nucleus of the Free Museum and Library which were established in Peel Park and opened to the public in January 1850. This was the first unconditionally free public library in Great Britain. Various alterations were made over the years and in 1937 the original house was demolished to make way for a new extention to the Museum. Lark Hill Place, the justly famous Victorian Street reconstruction now occupies its site. This view of the house was taken in 1868.

Peel Park was opened in 1846 and soon became and remained the obvious centre for exhibitions, displays and for the reception of visiting Royalty. It derives its name from Sir Robert Peel, the then Prime Minister who obtained the money through Parliament for its inception and who also made a large personal contribution towards its cost. A number of statues were erected in the park; this photograph shows that of Richard Cobden, the great Corn Law reformer, taken shortly after its inauguration in 1867. It is interesting to note the military guard which it was accorded. This statue along with others was removed from the park in 1954 and is now displayed in the grounds of Gawsworth Hall, Cheshire. In the background can be seen the gardens of Adelphi Street which formerly bordered the river.

In the early 1800's Salford's most distinguished road was the Crescent. Its large houses commanded splendid views over the land which was to become Peel Park and across the Irwell. This is a photograph of 1914 when the houses had long lost most of their aura and style but were still impressive in decline. The site of these two blocks of houses is now occupied by the A.E.U. offices and the Police Station.

Campbell's Flags in about the year 1900—Very different houses from those on the Crescent. This squalid tenement was in Davies Street, off Greengate. Almost unbelievably it was not demolished until 1911.

Campbell's Flags may have been an extreme example, but the large amount of sub-standard inadequate houses which existed in Salford was a certain guarantee of the success of the Public Wash House which opened in Hodge Lane on January 18th 1928. It contained 80 washing stalls and was felt to be the finest of its kind in the country.

The St. Ambrose' Boys Brigade Company (47th Manchester) walks past the Priory Hotel, High Street on a ceremonial parade. The boys in Sunday-best on the right of the picture look a little envious of the smart uniforms, but the year is 1913 and soon many of the older boys will be wearing uniforms in earnest and not in the streets of Salford.

As the First World War ground on, many Salford buildings were pressed into service as refugee centres, hospitals and the like. This is Langworthy Road School in 1916, temporarily converted into a military hospital. At a time when so many of Salford's young men were far from home, the hospital was obviously a great attraction to the young ladies of the district.

The vital importance of Salford Docks increased more than ever during the 1914-1918 war. It was not only supplies of food and essential materials that were landed here however. This photograph shows the arrival of a boat-load of American troops on October 18th 1918.

This photograph and the one on the facing page illustrate the widely different living styles in Edwardian Salford. Here, at Salisbury Croft, we see the end of one of Salford's many dock strikes on June 27th 1907. A vote has just been taken by a show of hands to return to work. Councillors Tom Fox and James Thomson have been successful in securing an improved pay award to the dockers for the very strenuous job of carrying timber. This increase brought their hourly rate of pay up to the princely sum of 8d. per hour.

Church workers at Claremont in 1908. Claremont was a handsome Georgian mansion which stood at the junction of the present Lullington and Buckland Roads. It became the home of the Heywood family, the well known bankers in 1821. The three Misses Heywood who were held in great affection for their very many charitable works and unfailing public-spiritedness are seen on the right of the picture.

In very marked contrast to the tranquility and grace of houses such as Claremont was the enormous bustle of Salford's Cattle Market in West High Street, seen here in 1906. It was opened in 1837 and closed in 1931 and during its lifetime it gave an incongruous country town atmosphere to part of the city.

This view of Claremont in 1898 gives an impression of the grandeur it possessed. It entertained such political notabilities as Lords Palmerston, Brougham and Russell. The large tree in the foreground was in fact planted by Lord Palmerston on a visit in 1856. When the house was demolished in the 1920's the Misses Heywood moved to another mansion known as Chaseley which formerly stood on the site of the present Salford Grammar School and renamed it Claremont. Thus Salford has had two Claremonts, a fact which still tends to confuse many Salfordians.

Broad Street Pendleton in about 1910. This area remained largely unchanged until its recent wholesale demolition. The Parish Church of St. Thomas on the right of the picture still remains of course, but the drinking fountain which was obviously a great attraction to thirsty boys on a hot summer's day has long since disappeared.

At the end of Broad Street stood the Woolpack, one of the most famous of Salford inns, splendidly positioned at the junction of Eccles Old Road and Bolton Road. This is a view of it in 1903 before its ornate timber front had been added. It was in use continuously as a public house from 1814 until its closure in 1967.

Trafford Road was originally known as South Cross Lane and was not of major importance. With the coming of the Manchester Ship Canal, the Docks, and the industrialisation of Trafford Park, however, towards the end of the last century it became and has remained a very busy thoroughfare. This is how it looked about the year 1907, remarkably little different from its appearance today. The Salisbury Hotel built in 1896, still fulfils its original function, but the tall building to its right has now become the Flying Angel Mission and the old Custom House to the right of that is now an annexe of Salford College of Technology.

One of the busiest road junctions in present-day Salford is the intersection of Cross Lane with Eccles New Road, Regent Road and Trafford Road. In this view of the bottom of Cross Lane in the early 1900's however, crossing the road appears to present few problems. The Palace Theatre on the left of the picture was opened in 1895, alternated somewhat erratically between operating as a theatre and as a cinema, and was finally destroyed by fire in January 1952. The Ship Hotel on the extreme left and the Drill Hall with its castellated tower still remain.

Regent Road has for a long time been the main shopping centre in the south east of the city. This is how it appeared in 1907. The view is towards Oldfield Road from just before the junction of Regent Road and Derby Street. The ornate Public Baths, opened in 1892, and one or two other buildings are all that remain of the scene today.

These canal cottages stood in Hampson Street close to its junction with East Ordsall Lane, and behind them lay the Manchester, Bolton and Bury Canal. The course of this undramatic waterway still threads through the city but it is often hidden from the eye of the casual observer. The cottages were pulled down not long after this photograph of 1906 and their site is now occupied by David Brown's Engineering Works.

In 1835 the first Methodist church and Sunday School services in Irlams o th'Height were held in these cottages on Bolton Road. They were the homes of Charles Waring and James Raikes and were demolished to make way for the Height Methodist Church which was proudly opened on April 127th 1878. This is a view of 1875 and it is interesting to note that Johnson's ironmonger's still bearing the same name has only recently been closed. Now the church itself is to disappear on account of road widening.

Aerial views in 1930 were not common and a particular interest attaches to this one and that on the opposite page. Chapel Street runs across the centre of the picture. Salford Royal Hospital and St. Philip's Church can be seen on the left, Salford Cathedral in the centre, Bexley Square and the Town Hall on the right. Near the top right hand corner is St. Stephen's Church, a late 18th century building which was taken down in 1957. Very dense housing on both sides of Chapel Street had for many years crowded the civic and ecclesiastical centres of the city.

This is the classic face of Salford as the world outside has come to know it.—Lower Broughton in 1930 shows tremendously high-density building and a completely haphazard juxtaposition of house and factory. We are looking north along the Irwell from Adelphi. Great Clowes Street runs along the top right hand corner of the picture with Adelphi Street and Silk Street veering right to Broughton Bridge. At the top left we can just make out the shop fronts of Lower Broughton Road.

Salford has always been a place of small shops rather than of large department stores on the Manchester pattern. This was Nelson's butcher's in Trafford Road in 1909. Mr. Samuel Nelson is the bowler-hatted figure in the doorway.

Mr. Richard Horner stands with his wife and daughter at the door of his cobbler's shop., No. 15, Lissadel Street. The date is somewhere between 1914 and 1916.

At 338 and 338A Liverpool Street, Mrs. Margaret Southwood combined the unlikely joint business of newsagent and tripe dealer, and in this view of about 1905 her small army of newsboys is assembled in front of the shop. On the left of the picture is Mrs. Southwood's son, the father of Mr. William Southwood, whose own newsagents—a few yards from this original shop is now being demolished.

An ideal photograph from the historian's point of view. The name and number of the shop are quite visible and as a special bonus the poster announcing the engagement of Winston Churchill enables us to pinpoint the date as Saturday August 15th 1908. The additional fact that it is the 6 a.m. edition of the 'Morning Express' which is advertised indicates that the picture was taken during the earlier part of the day. This is No. 106, Cross Lane, obviously a high-class stationer's. The shop, now a newsagent's still stands next to the Buck Hotel.

A most interesting photograph of Salford Docks soon after the opening of the Manchester Ship Canal in 1894. The contrast between the modern looking steamship and the stately grace of the sailing ship 'Ellida' with its intricate pattern of masts and rigging is very striking. The Ellida was used to transport timber, and its unloaded cargo can be seen on the wharf.

The opening of the Manchester Ship Canal in 1894 had perhaps the most far-reaching importance of any event in Salford's history. This triumphal arch, expressive of splendid civic pride was erected at the eastern end of Regent Road, near to Oldfield Road, to commemorate the occasion. Through the archway can be seen the tower of the old Regent Road Library.

A man drives his pony and trap with nonchalant ease along the middle of a deserted Trafford Road in the early 1890's, but with the coming of the Trafford Park industrial estate the days for this kind of thing are numbered. This is a view from near the iron bridge over the Irwell which was built in 1878. When the new swing bridge over the Slip Canal was opened in 1894, the river was diverted.

Any·occasion which brought a splash of colour to life was always welcome to the ordinary people of Salford, and a Royal visit was sure to bring out the crowds even when, as on this occasion it was only of 45 minutes duration. The date is July 13th 1913 and King George V and Queen Mary together with Lord Derby and the glittering ranks of the 1st Life Guards are approaching Salford Cathedral in their journey along Chapel Street towards Manchester.

In the absence of a royal occasion the annual church anniversary provided a splendid opportunity for dressing up and display as well as the chance of expressing the great loyalty and devotion which very many people felt for their own church or chapel. This is St. Thomas's Pendleton anniversary on May 2nd 1909, and the procession is moving down Church street. The church on the left is the Mother of God and St. James Roman Catholic Church, now isolated in the complex of the new Salford Shopping Centre.

St Thomas's Church Anniversary. May 2nd 1909. 4.

The Salford Working Girls' Institute opened in 1903 and aimed to provide instruction in such practical subjects as cooking, sewing, laundering, dressmaking, and sick-nursing. It fulfilled a very real need for girls who had little time or opportunity for more than the most basic education. These young ladies appear to be practising various aspects of housewifery and the happy atmosphere of the place is quite apparent. The building was situated in Huddart Street, off Regent Road, close to the site of the old Infantry Barracks. It was destroyed by enemy action during the last war.

Salford's two most outstanding remaining old buildings are Kersal Cell and Ordsall Hall. Kersal Cell, seen here in 1890 was owned for a long time by the Byrom family, but contrary to popular belief John Byrom did not write the words of the famous hymn 'Christians Awake' here. It is in parts the oldest building in the city, its basic 16th century structure embodying at its core the remains of a 12th century Cluniac monastery, although it was flawed by unsuitable alterations during the 19th century. It is now used as a country club.

This view of Ordsall Hall in 1875 presents a very different picture from the beautifully restored building which has recently been opened as a museum. Connected with the Radclyffe family for over 300 years its glory is its 15th century Great Hall. During the 19th century it suffered many vicissitudes. Its mediaeval timbered construction was covered over and at various times it was used as a working-men's club and as a clergy training school. At the time of this photograph it was still in a semi-rural setting, but the tide of industrial housing which surrounded it by the end of the century was soon to commence.

The Turnpike roads and their consequent toll bars were features of Salford life from the middle of the 18th century until towards the end of the 19th. This is the toll bar at the junction of Eccles Old Road and Bolton Road, looking towards Pendleton. The toll was abolished in 1872 not long before the date of this picture.

The end of the Turnpike era and the freeing from toll charges of important bridges such as that at Broughton, allowed trading centres in Salford to develop and expand. Lower Broughton Road has for many years been one of the busiest shopping thoroughfares in the Broughton area of the city. This is a view of it in 1921. The buildings on the right of the road have changed little today. Of those on the left, the busy fruiterers has gone and the Co-operative store, with clock, is now a wallpaper shop. The three public houses, Beehive, Poets' Corner and Royal Archer remain, although the Poets' Corner has now lost its turret and weather-vane.

This picture of 1905 is of Brown's farm which stood in New River Street, Weaste, At this time it was the home of James Henry Brown, farmer and meat salesman. Surprisingly it was not demolished until 1921.

Salford is not usually associated with agriculture, but there were in fact quite a number of farms within the city boundaries well within living memory. This is New Hall Farm photographed in 1899. It was also known as Higson's Farm from the name of one of its occupants in the mid-nineteenth century. It stood on the site of the present Blandford Road, off Gerald Road and was obviously a building of considerable antiquity. It became a butcher's in 1900 and was demolished in 1920.

This is no ordinary farm. It is in fact Kersal Hall, which like Kersal Cell was owned at one time by the Byrom family. It stood on Littleton Road, at its junction with Moor Lane, and was a place of enormous interest. Despite being one of the best examples of 16th century building in this part of the country, it was demolished in 1937 to make way for a housing estate. It was in use as a farm for many years until 1935. This view of the rear of the building, architecturally its best part, was taken about 1900.

For entertainment and excitement in Salford there was little to compare with Race Day. The most famous course was at Castle Irwell, but from 1867 until 1901 it was situated at New Barns, which was on the site of the present No. 9 Dock. This was the scene in Trafford Road in or about 1894 when a wonderful variety of vehicles assembled to take the race crowds home. Salisbury's Buildings on the left of the picture are easily recognisable.

A view inside the New Barns race-course on May 31st 1901, the last occasion on which a meeting was held there. The extension of the Docks necessitated its closure and the new course at Castle Irwell was opened in the following year.

Kersal Moor was another big attraction for city dwellers on a fine Sunday or Bank Holiday. In this photograph of 1901 Mrs Esther Orrett, then aged 22 pauses to have her picture taken, In the background is the old artificial lake. The moor which has yielded several interesting prehistoric finds, was purchased by Salford Corporation as an open space in 1936.

One of the most favourite forms of outing, of course, was the pub picnic, and here we have a real vintage example—Ma Willoughby's picnic of 1920. Ma Willoughby was the licensee of the Prince of Wales Feathers on Windsor Bridge, a pub which has only disappeared in recent years. She sits at the centre of her admiring clientele, looking superbly capable of exercising unquestioned authority over any and every one of them.

The last photograph celebrates an important municipal occasion—the linking of Pendleton with Broughton by the opening of the new Littleton Road Bridge on August 9th 1905. The cost of its construction was £11,000 and this cost was borne entirely by Captain Clowes, Lord of the Manor. The ceremonial celebrations were held at the County Stand of Castle Irwell race-course. The aristocratic figures of Captain Clowes and his wife are easily distinguishable in the centre of the picture. So too is the Mayor, Sir William Stephens in his chain of office. Around them are grouped what must must have been the cream of the Salford Establishment of that time. The members of the Salford Police Band assembled behind them to provide a final civic flourish.